Live to Win

My Victory Over Cancer

Live to Win
My Victory Over Cancer
Altovise Ferguson

Live To Win
My Victory Over Cancer

by

Altovise Ferguson

Live to Win; My Victory Over Cancer

Copyright 2013 © Altovise Ferguson

All rights reserved. This book or parts thereof may not be reproduced in any form, distributed, stored in a retrieval system, or transmitted in any form by any means - electronic, mechanical, photocopy, recording, or otherwise - without prior written permission of the copyright owner and/or publisher, except as provided by United States of America copyright law.

Published by
Scribe Publications, Inc.
219-644-8981
www.spub.biz

Cover design by Bernard Granger

Unless otherwise identified, scripture quotations are from the Holy Bible King James Version. Used by permission. All rights reserved.

Scripture quotations marked AMP are taken from the Amplified Bible, Copyright (c) 1954, 1958, 1962, 1964, 1965, 1987 by The Lockman Foundation. Used by permission. (www.Lockman.org).

Scripture quotations noted NLT are from the Holy Bible, New Living Translation. Copyright (c) 1996 and 2004. Used by permission of Tyndale House Publishers, Wheaton, Illinois. 60190. All rights reserved.

Scripture quotations noted MSG are from the The Message. Copyright © 1993, 1994, 1995, 1996, 2000, 2001, 2002. Used by permission of NavPress Publishing Group.

Scripture quotations noted NIV are from Holy Bible, New International Version®, NIV® Copyright © 1973, 1978, 1984, 2011 by Biblica, Inc.® Used by permission. All rights reserved worldwide.

Any name referencing satan will not be given the respect of capitalization, even at the risk of improper sentence structure.

ISBN-13: 978-0-9967824-1-8

Library of Congress Control Number: 2015951655

Printed in the United States of America

Dedication

This book is dedicated to anyone battling any challenge in life, especially sickness or disease. Healing is yours.

Acknowledgements

First, I would like to thank my Lord & Savior Jesus Christ for loving me, healing me, and protecting me through it all. To my husband Archie Ferguson Jr., thank you for loving me and never leaving my side. To my mother, Madeline Bailey, your warfare prayers and care of our precious babies Amari and Ahmad were invaluable.

I want to thank my "Papa" Douglas Armmer for being a loving, patient, praying father to me. Terry Armmer, my TeTe, thank you for coming every day, praying for me and just giving of yourself as you always do. To my grandmother, the late Mary Dee Burns, you gave me so much love and made sure I was comfortable and well taken care of. To my sisters Dawn, Jamila, Lashouna, Lorraine and Jacqeulyn, you all stood and showered me with so much love and support. To Aunt Tina Salter and the late Tammy Burns, you are the best aunts a girl can have.

To my sister Paula and her husband Alphonzo Rogers, you were right there in the beginning, taking care of my kids and you gave of yourself in every way. I am so grateful to have you in my life. To my sister Kimberly and her husband Chris Brown, you have been my rock; you were always there. I am blessed to be your sister.

To the Ferguson and Cheatum family, thank you for your visits, calls and prayers. To Apostle Meredith and Dr. Marilyn Shackelford and An Open Door Church family, your prayers and your support will never be forgotten. Apostle Meredith & Dr. Marilyn Shackelford, you are two of the most awesome anointed pastors. You taught me the word of God, how to stand and to never give up. To Drs. Cedric & Joyce Oliver and the Embassies of Christ family... You taught me about my purpose in life, how to reach my destiny, how stand in faith and how with God, I am unstoppable. Thank you.

To Dr. Mildred C. Harris, you spoke this book into existence when I didn't know I had the capability to write a book. Thank you for your unending obedience to God.

To my manager Anita Hawkins and my assistant Tavetta Patterson…Both of you prayed, believed, and pushed me. Let's continue this journey to bless God's people.

To Dr. Geoffery Dixon, Dr. V. Vyas, Methodist hospitals and staff, I was shown so much love, encouragement and support. To Dr. B.H. Barai and staff, I have never met a doctor who not only is gifted but also cares about every aspect of his patient's life. Dr. Barai you were truly sent by God to take care of me.

Table of Contents

FOREWORD	13
INTRODUCTION	14
CHAPTER 1 BUSY WIFE, BUSY LIFE	17
CHAPTER 2 STORM ON THE HORIZON	26
CHAPTER 3 DEVASTATED THROUGH DREAMS	33
CHAPTER 4 LOOKING IN THE FACE OF DEATH	40
CHAPTER 5 TURMOIL TURNED TO TRIUMPH	59
CONFESSION	72
DAILY AFFIRMATIONS	72
PRAYER OF SALVATION	73

Foreword

"Be it done unto you according to your faith."

It is so beautiful to watch a Christian grow in their faith walk with God. I watched God take Altovise through some of the darkest times in her life and with each attack of the enemy; I witnessed the evolution of a warrior as she fought for her health, the welfare of her family, her peace of mind, but more importantly, her faith in God. Through every trial and set back, her faith in the Word grew. She relied totally on the Father and His faithfulness to her brought her victory over the works of the enemy.

If you want to be encouraged, revived and energized, this book is for you. Read and let your faith rise to new levels.

Love you Vise!

Quintin Jarrett

Introduction

Whatever you are facing, I would like to speak healing over you right now. Father I thank You that the faith of everyone that reads this book will explode to new heights in You. They will believe that You are the God of miracles! In Jesus name, I speak to every diagnosis of cancer and any disease and command it to dry up and die.

No matter what the diagnosis is, you will not be afraid. The enemy is defeated in Jesus name; his plans, schemes, and assignments are canceled in Jesus' name. You are healed.

Joshua 1:9 (NIV)

Have I not commanded you? Be strong and courageous. Do not be afraid; do not be discouraged, for the LORD your God will be with you wherever you go.

Making a decision to survive is totally up to a person's will to live. It is the same as making a decision of what to wear or what to eat for dinner. If making the choice to live, you must lean on the Word to help you keep the faith and keep fighting no matter what you see, hear or think. Survivors keep progressing forward in the face of opposition and find a way to thrive beyond what they have survived.

A diagnosis should not determine whether you survive, but unfortunately far too many people allow the diagnosis to dictate what they believe is possible; their decision to live is based on what they have been told in a medical report. I chose to take a different path. I made a decision to live based on the Word of God and His promises of healing (Psalm 107:20), health (Proverbs 4:22) and long life (Psalm 91:16). I decided to live for my destiny and my family. Even though I had not received the manifestation of what I confessed and believed, I knew God was faithful to His Word and could be trusted. I developed a will to fight until I received what I desired, which was healing. If I can do it, then so can you.

John 10:10 (Amp)

The thief comes only in order to steal kill and destroy. I came that they may have and enjoy life and have it in abundance, to the full, till it overflows.

How many times have you seen someone who looks well, skin is beautiful, body looks physically fit, and everything seems fine? Then all of a sudden, you may hear they are sick or even near death. Puzzling isn't it? Sadly, this is the story for so many people, including me. That's why it is so important to pray continuously and speak the Word over your life when everything appears to be going well. You never know what plan of attack the enemy is plotting against you, but do not fear or be discouraged, Jesus, our great intercessor is at the right hand of God the Father praying for you. Just as Jesus told Peter satan desired to sift him as wheat but He had already prayed that Peter's faith fail not (Luke 22:31-32), so too is Jesus praying for you, that your faith fail not. Notice Jesus did not pray that the attacks of satan will be stopped or that Peter would not go through the attacks from the enemy but Jesus prayed for Peter's ***FAITH***! Jesus may not take you out of the situation, but you can be sure that He has already prayed for you and your faith and because Jesus is the author and finisher of your faith (Hebrews 12:2), you are guaranteed to win!

Chapter 1
Busy Wife, Busy Life

The year 2002 proved to be a blessed but busy year for my family and me. My marriage to Archie was still new; the ink had not dried on our marriage license! We had less than a year under our belts but were enjoying our married life. As a hair stylist, God had really blessed me with a great clientele. My family and my friends, especially Paula and Kim, we extremely supportive in all my endeavors, which were many. Theatre, dancing, singing, modeling, hair and make-up artist…..there was not much that I wasn't doing. I loved it all. Now add to this mix me being with child…I was pregnant with our second child, a baby boy!

During my second trimester, I experienced severe pain in my lower left side of my back. The pain began to travel down my left leg, causing an intensely sharp and shooting pain. My OB/GYN thought the baby could have been sitting in a position that pressed on a nerve so I overlooked it because the pain, although severe, was never constant.

On July 1 at approximately 9:20 p.m., I gave birth to our son. Although I did not have a caesarean or major complications, this delivery was hard, much harder than when my daughter, Amari was born. She weighed eight pounds, ten ounces and it was difficult, but my son was much more difficult. While he was smaller than my daughter was, only six pounds, fourteen ounces, the pain and experience was worse. Even on the next day, my doctor came in and talked to me about the delivery. Typically, mothers are sent home one day after childbirth. My hospital stay was about three days so that is an indicator of how rough this delivery was.

  My body never fully recovered after the birth of our son. Naturally I was exhausted, but I seemed extremely exhausted…more than the normal exhaustion from giving birth. Though I was not 100% myself, I decided to return to work in September; my clients were both happy that I was back but also wanted to make sure I was well enough to resume styling hair. I had planned to return after my six-week check-up but my body just would not let me. Somehow, I found the strength to push through the exhaustion to resume life, as I had known it. Back to work, back to my busy schedule. I made no time for myself. Everything was about everyone else and I was last. I was raised to put other people's needs ahead of mine but I would soon learn that there needed to be a balance.

  Soon after I returned to work, I began singing again. I also began working in a musical with a community theatre in the city. Additionally, I was very active at church; my church was everything to me. I had been totally committed to God for about four years now and my relationship with Him was growing stronger each day. I was doing what God had called and anointed me to do through the grace of God. Having a solid and stable foundation in the Word of God is what sustained me. I also had an outstanding support system. My "village" was made of my mother, my aunt, close friends and relatives. While I was involved in quite of bit of activities, my primary focus was my family.

A few months had passed since the birth of our son, but my body still did not feel right. In December 2002, as I was preparing to go to the salon, I felt an unusual mass in my neck and began to wonder what those huge lumps were. "Ouch Lord. What is going on with my neck?" is what I began to think. As a singer, this was a big issue. The pain was so severe that I could not carry a note. I was forced to take a break from singing. These lumps were large and very painful. I began to wear scarves to cover them up, as they were quite visible. It was easier to wear scarves than having to answer questions from people constantly ask me about the lumps. I thought that maybe the lumps could have been the result of me gritting my teeth too hard while in labor, thus messing up the root canal I had when I was in high school.

I began to confess the Word of God over my body. In addition to speaking the Word, I began to treat this with natural remedies. I used herbal teas and natural remedies for the throat that I purchased at a health food store. Many say that home remedies and natural cures are good for the soul but God's Word is truly the best.

Proverbs 4:20 – 23 (Amp)

My son, attend to My words; consent and submit to My sayings. Let them not depart from your sight; keep them in the center of your heart. For they are life to those who find them, healing and health to all their flesh. Keep and guard your heart with all vigilance and above all that you guard, for out of it flow the springs of life.

Within a month, the symptoms went away. Hallelujah! However, my celebration was short lived. Two months later, they returned. When I went to the doctor, he told me that it was my lymph nodes and that meant I had an infection in my body. He prescribed me antibiotics and said that I would be fine. Well I ended up going right back to the ER about three weeks later and the doctor told me that I needed dental work. He believed that since the tooth cap had come off and exposed the rotten tooth that was left from that root canal, the bacteria that had been lying dormant had caused my glands to swell, eventually leading to a leakage that drained into my throat. I went to the dentist to take care of the issue.

A few weeks later, the pain and lumps returned. While at church on a Sunday morning, I decided to go up for prayer and ask them to be in agreement with me concerning my healing.

James 5:14 – 15 (NLT)

Are any of you sick? You should call for the elders of the church to come and pray over you, anointing you with oil in the name of the Lord. Such a prayer offered in faith will heal the sick, and the Lord will make you well.

At times, you may need to call on reinforcement to join forces with you while you are fighting. This does not diminish your faith at all. The Word tells us *if two of you shall agree on earth as touching anything that they ask, it shall be done for them of My Father which is in heaven* (Matthew 18:19). I stood in faith, believing that I was made whole. The scriptures that anchored my faith were Isaiah 53:5 (Amp – *But He was wounded for our transgressions, He was bruised for our guilt and iniquities, the chastisement (needful to obtain) peace and well being for us was upon Him and with the stripes that wounded Him we are healed and made whole)* and Jeremiah 32:27 (*Behold I am the Lord, the God of all flesh. Is there anything too hard for me?*).

I had faith and trusted God's Word so being a Spirit-filled Christian who attended a faith-filled ministry, of course I said, "*I am healed by His stripes.*" I truly believe that we should confess the Word of God no matter what the situation looks like.

Hebrews 10:23

Let us hold fast the profession of our faith without wavering; for He is faithful that promised.

My belief was that I was already healed, so I went on my merry little way with no concern about what was going on in my body; my faith was locked and settled on healing. I knew it was only a matter of time before it would manifest. I knew if I said what I saw through the eyes of faith, then I would eventually see what I said in the natural.

During a Wednesday night service at my church, I had just finished singing and was getting ready to sit down and immediately my back began to hurt so bad; it felt as if someone was hitting my back with a hammer. Still trying to avoid going to the hospital, my mother and husband forced me to go. The emergency room doctor said it was muscle spasms and gave me pain medication. That worked for a couple of days, but soon I was back in pain.

Even though I was in excruciating pain, I still worked in the salon. I kept my painful struggles hidden so that no one knew what I was experiencing. You know *"Superwoman"* could not show any signs of weakness! I was too busy trying to be everything to everyone; I was of the mindset that I *must* get this done, I *must* get that done. I just kept pushing myself through the pain. One morning while at work, I started to feel a tingling sensation and numbness throughout the lower part of my body. It seemed as if I was paralyzed so I called my husband and told him what was going on with me. We immediately went back to the emergency room. This was my third emergency room visit within a month and this time. Now the doctor suggested I see a neurologist. I knew something was seriously wrong.

I was tired, extremely fatigued, but still playing life. I remember one particular morning, my husband kept calling home, and I did not answer the phone. I was still sleep and it was almost noon. I was awfully late for work that day. The kids were awake and moving about the house but I just did not have the energy to tend to them. Archie was upset that I did not answer the phone but

I just flat out told him I was tired. At first, he was not listening; then he said, "What's really going on with you?" I responded, "I don't know." At that point, both he and I were starting to get concerned.

Chapter 2
Storm on the Horizon

With my health facing these challenges, that should have been a warning sign for me to not only get a thorough examination done from head to toe but to also slow down and take time for myself. Yet, I continued to ignore the signs. The red lights were flashing, indicating **DANGER AHEAD** but I never gave heed to them. The pain was trying to tell me something, but I did not slow down enough to listen.

I thought 2001 and 2002 were busy years for me. As I look back, 2003 would be one for the books. I had been married for nearly two years and was the proud mother of two beautiful children, one daughter and one son. I was focused on my job as a cosmetologist. I loved what I did. It was truly a God-given gift that allowed me to touch so many people and to share with them God's love and care.

In addition to being a hair stylist, I was also actively pursuing my greatest passion, which is arts and entertainment. I was getting ready for a musical with a community theatre group. I was a part of a community ensemble cast for the play Joseph and the Technicolor Dreamcoat. I was slated to star as the narrator. I was also in a gospel singing group, as well as singing at my church. Things were looking bright for my future.

At that time, I thought all these activities were fine because I was utilizing the gifts and talents God had given me to bless and help others. Little did I realize that I did not know how to balance my life in regards to taking care of me. I felt that at 26, I should be busy; it was my job to see about everyone else. I was shown through the examples of the women in my family that if others are happy, then I am happy. The women in my family always put themselves last. My grandmother raised me and not only was she my maternal grandmother to me but she was a like a mother to me. I watched how she worked every day, making sure everything was fine for our family. She hardly ever got any sleep, let alone time for herself, but she seemed content in this. As I got older, I realized Mama needed time for herself. See I **said** I would do things differently but I found myself starting to do the same thing as Mama. In my mind, it was ok because I thought I had the strength of 10 women. I can do it A-L-L….or so I believed. Boy was I wrong! Just like Mama, I still needed time for myself.

On the outside, I looked fine but on the inside, I was a mess. Emotionally and mentally, I was hurting from the pains of the past. I loved Archie and loved being his wife, yet my marriage was suffering because I was a ticking time bomb. I walked into the marriage as a wounded and broken person. When we got married, I was still harboring and clinging onto old unresolved issues in my heart. Prior to our marriage, we had a child together and Archie had a daughter from a previous relationship. I had not truly forgiven; with my mouth, I said "I forgive you" but in my heart, I still had animosity, which was turning into bitterness.

We had no idea how to work together in a marriage. Yes, we were both Christians, loved God, and went through pre-marital counseling, but what does that mean. You may be given information but until it is applied, it does little good to just know it.

I became good at faking it. I had no real peace. I had manufactured joy and played the role enough to fool most people, but deep inside, I was in pain and crying out for help. I felt so disconnected at one point in my marriage of less than two years that I said Lord if I got sick, would Archie love me? Now I did not have a clue what I was even allowing to be released into the atmosphere.

Proverbs 18:21(Amp)

Death and life are in the power of the tongue, and they who indulge in it shall eat the fruit of it [for death or life].

You cannot allow pain, hurt, issues or challenges to allow us to confess or speak things that are negative or just plain foolish. The enemy prowls around looking for ammunition to use against you, so do not give it to him!

Even with the compounded physical and emotional pains, I was still juggling church, family and work. Weight was dropping from my body fast. I was excited because naturally, I wanted all the pregnancy weight gone, but it was coming off extremely fast. Once the run of the show had ended, I got a personal trainer to help me tone my body. After our first session, she told me to go to a doctor immediately and that she would not continue to train me until I did. I could not do any lifting without screaming in pain. I could do no back exercises at all, and core exercises were out of the question. *What is really going on?*

Despite the pain and questions, I maintained a positive attitude. I made up in my mind that whatever this was attacking my body had a fight on its hands; it was not going down without a fight to the finish.

There was a Wednesday night when I was ministering as the praise and worship leader at our church's newly launched ministry location in Gary, Indiana. As I sang each note, pain hit me harder and harder in my back (this was an indicator of the level of warfare that was to come). When I finished, I sat down crying and praying all at the same time. My husband and my mom came to my side. They began to pray and the pain began to leave so I kept on moving, handling business as usual because, as you know, with a five-month-old son and six-year-old daughter, there was never a dull moment.

As time went on, the lumps in my neck did not go away so I figured it was time to really take this serious and get checked out by a doctor (not just in the ER). So many church folks feel guilty, or even worse, condemn people for going to the doctor or taking medicine. **THE DEVIL IS A LIAR!** If your level of faith is to believe God for total healing without taking medicines or going to the doctor, then do not condemn others who decide to take a different path. If you are truly a person of faith, **PRAY** for them!

The doctor had given me some medicines that would address the pain. I had some relief from the pain but it was short-lived. Outside of discomfort and irritation, the lumps also affected my singing and vocal range. I was forced to drop down an octave when I was well enough to sing.

Eventually, it began to feel like my strength was being sapped from my body. Tired, tired, and tired! That is how I started to feel but me being the Superwoman that I convinced myself that

I was, I foolishly kept on going with my intense work and stage schedule. I thought to myself maybe I was tired from breastfeeding our son or from being so active in theatre or from doing hair or from being a wife and mother. I was trying to find any and every possible reason for why I was feeling like this. However, there was something deeper going on with me. I needed to get to root of the issue. The extreme fatigue and night sweats made it nearly unbearable. Eventually, whatever this was began to affect me in other ways. I started moving at a slower pace and at times would completely lose my balance. "Lord what is going on here?"

Chapter 3
Devastated through Dreams

Throughout the Bible, God used dreams to communicate a message to people. Joseph, Daniel, John, Paul and others had dreams or interpreted dreams to convey what God wanted to tell people. Whether good or bad, dreams are a very powerful tool that can let you know what could happen. Dreams can very well become one's reality.

In Genesis 41, Pharaoh had a dream that he did not understand. This caused him to be very troubled because none of his top advisors and wise men could give the interpretation. God had favored Joseph to interpret the dreams of the chief butler and chief baker while they were in prison together. The butler remembered this and told Pharaoh that he knew someone who could help. In walks Joseph. Again, God favored Joseph to interpret the dreams. There would be seven years of plenty in Egypt and seven years of famine. Because of this, they were able to prepare for the famine that was to come. Had they ignored the warnings from the dreams, the entire nation would have been consumed by the famine.

Well I had a similar experience. I had two dreams. In the first dream, I had seen my own funeral. I woke up in a cold sweat. It seemed so real; I could not shake the feeling and imagery. I began praying and binding the enemy. In the second dream, I was coming out of a clinic or doctor's office crying. It was as if I was given a bad report. I saw my family crying and in turmoil. My children were calling for me. My husband was in a daze and again, I saw my own funeral. I woke up shaking, but I ignored it. These dreams should have been an awakening for me, but I stayed asleep. I still did not seek medical attention for myself, as I should have. The enemy was trying to make these dreams my reality and my ignorance was helping him.

Hebrews 12:25 (Amp)

"So see to it that you do not reject Him or refuse to listen to and heed Him Who is speaking to you now. For if they (the Israelites) did not escape when they refused to listen and heed Him Who warned and divinely instructed them (here) on earth (revealing with heavenly warning His will), how much less shall we escape if we reject and turn our backs on Him Who cautions and admonishes us from heaven?"

Hebrews 12:25 The Message (MSG)

So don't turn a deaf ear to these gracious words. If those who ignored earthly warnings didn't get away with it, what will happen to us if we turn our backs on heavenly warnings? His voice that time shook the earth to its foundations; this time—he's told us this quite plainly—he'll also rock the heavens: "One last shaking, from top to bottom, stem to stern."

"The phrase one last shaking means a thorough housecleaning, getting rid of all the historical and religious junk so that the unshakable essentials stand clear and uncluttered."[1]

Like a fool, I kept going on as if nothing was bothering me. I turned a deaf ear and in essence, nearly rejected the warnings from the dreams. My focus and concentration was on this play. I was giving it my all during rehearsals and ended up losing my voice. Because I never fully recovered, during the performances I had to drop the songs a full octave. I asked again, "God what's going on?" Doors of opportunity were opening for me. Why was I going through this?

I decided to see my gynecologist. You may be wondering why the gynecologist. Well the pain I was experiencing was going from my spine and travelling into my vaginal area. The doctor asked me how I cut hair. I thought that was an odd question but he explained that the pain in could be due to the way I held my tools, how I was positioning my body and the length of time I was on my feet. I did not realize my posture could have contributed to the pain. He decided not to speculate but to give me a series of tests.

While waiting on the test results, I started falling while I walked. I would walk to the car and just fall on my face. Then the unexpected happened; I started becoming temporarily paralyzed from the waist down. Once I regained mobility, I could not walk without the aid of holding onto things or a cane. It was horrible, but I continued to work. Can you believe that I continued working? I was forced to cut my workload in half. I hired a person to help me at work; she shampooed my clients. I was determined not to let whatever this was shut me down. I borrowed a cane from my step dad and began using it.

Eventually I had to have someone tell me what to do because I was not listening. One evening, my friend and fellow stylist Kim had called to see why I was not going to get checked out and she found out that I was at work. She got in touch with my husband and they both came to my job. I had just finished my last client when they arrived. Both of them fussed at me about being there and demanded that I go to the hospital immediately. I tried to tell them that I was fine but they kept insisting I go. Knowing that

I was not going to win, I gave in and went with my husband to the hospital.

Once there, the attending doctor ran a diagnostic test on me. He told me to close my eyes and lay on my back; he began to stick my legs with little needles like acupuncture. I did not feel anything. He asked repeatedly as he added more needles, "Do you feel that?" I said, "No." Archie said, "Baby are you sure you don't feel that?" Once again, I answered, "No." I could not see what the doctor was doing because he put a sheet up that covered the bottom part of my body and told me to close my eyes. Had I known what he was doing, I probably would have tried to run out the room! Once done, he told me that I needed to see a neurologist. We found a neurologist, but he could not see me until September so I had to suffer through this for another month.

I continued my duties as a wife and mother. I was ignorant and thought that taking time to care for myself was a sin. I did not think that things would be ok with my family if I took a day off. In reality, life would continue whether I am there or not there.

By this time, the situation was growing worse; I was right back in the ER. I had been there multiple times since the doctor's visit this month. They told me I had inflammation in my spine and gave me morphine injections. Although the morphine did help with pain management, it did not last long. I only had brief relief from the pain. The morphine was not enough to make me pain free. When it wore off, I felt excruciating pain surging throughout my body.

Chapter 4
Looking in the Face of Death

Looking in the Face of Death

My body began to shut down. I was not getting any better. I tried to convince myself that I was ok, but my body showed something different. The next couple of days involved extensive testing. I spent my 27th birthday in the hospital. WOW... what a way to celebrate. Just when I thought one of my worst birthdays could not get any worse, I was proven wrong. The next day, August 14, I found out that I had a massive tumor on my spine that needed to be removed immediately. The doctor said if it were not removed, I would never walk again. What? Never walk again? A tumor? Where did it come from? All these thoughts ran through my mind. I did not have time to get a second opinion; I had to move fast. I was placed in the hands of the neurosurgeon, who was a young African American man who looked to be my age. They told me that the tumor was not cancerous, but I would have to learn to walk all over again. What? Would I be just like a baby, not being able to do things for myself? It was just too much but I remembered the scripture, I Peter 5:7 (Amp), about casting all my cares, worries, anxieties upon Him

Casting the whole of your care [all your anxieties, all your worries, all your concerns, once and for all] on Him, for He cares for you affectionately and cares about you watchfully.

I stood on that. I had to meditate on the Word of God for what I was about to face. I could not listen to others or even family that maybe had different opinions about how I should handle the situation.

Psalm 1:1-2 (Amp)

Blessed (happy, fortunate, prosperous, and enviable) is the man who walks and lives not in the counsel of the ungodly [following their advice, their plans and purposes], nor stands [submissive and inactive] in the path where sinners walk, nor sits down [to relax and rest] where the scornful [and the mockers] gather. But his delight and desire are in the law of the Lord, and on His law (the precepts, the instructions, the teachings of God) he habitually meditates (ponders and studies) by day and by night.

August 19, 2003 was a Monday morning and I had to be transferred from the Methodist Northlake campus to the Southlake campus. The surgery lasted about four hours, which was a little longer than expected. When I came out of surgery, I was placed on the intensive care unit floor, where I would remain for about a week. Once I was awake, the neurosurgeon came to tell me that the tumor did not look right and that it needed to be sent off for testing. I thank God I was not left in the dark, so I really was not apprehensive or worried about the tumor. I was just ready to walk again!

After a week in the ICU, I was quickly moved to the rehabilitation floor to start rehab and I mean I was in full force rehab immediately. I had rehab three times a day and I was lifting weights the first day! It was so difficult that I became overwhelmed. The challenging part was standing for the first time. I really thought I could still walk. I know this might sound ridiculous, but I thought that when I stood up, I would be stiff but still able to walk somewhat. I had already told my clients I would be returning to work by October so I knew I had to get going, but reality hit me hard like a ton of bricks.

I stood for the first time about four weeks after rehab and I shook uncontrollably all over and flopped right back down to the chair. Oh my God, it was just unreal. I could not believe I was just like a child. My legs and thighs felt like liquid. It seemed like there was no muscle mass at all. My nurse asked me what was wrong. I told her I am facing the reality that I have to learn to walk all over again and it was mind blowing. She explained to me that spinal or any back surgery is serious and should not be taken lightly. She told me it was going to take time for me to heal and I was going to have to work very hard in rehab.

I was the youngest patient in rehab. There were mostly older people, amputees, people who had been ill and hadn't moved in a while and others who had surgery like me. I was determined to move! Every day I would stand and take steps little by little and I began to really see that I would walk again, I would dance again, and yes I would wear heels again! The scriptures Philippians 4:13 and Isaiah 41:10 began ringing in my spirit and I just stood on them.

Philippians 4:13(Amp)

I have strength for all things in Christ Who empowers me [I am ready for anything and equal to anything through Him Who infuses inner strength into me; I am [self-sufficient in Christ's sufficiency].

Isaiah 41:10 (Amp)

Fear not [there is nothing to fear], for I am with you; do not look around you in terror and be dismayed, for I am your God. I will strengthen and harden you to difficulties, yes, I will help you; yes, I will hold you up and retain you with My [victorious] right hand of rightness and justice.

Looking in the Face of Death

Fear and doubt came straight from the enemy to get me to focus on the current situation. The enemy, which is any spirit that is contrary to God and His spirit of peace and love, comes to steal, kill and destroy. According to John 10:10 that is his job so we should not be surprised when negative things rise up to attack us. Through prayer and patience, we must stay on our job of *fighting the good fight of faith* (1 Timothy 6:12). Victories are won in life through prayer, fasting, and meditating on the Word of God. And after doing all of this, stand in faith (Ephesians 6:13) and believe by focusing on what the Word of God tells you and not the facts of what your situation is trying to tell you.

Isaiah 35:4

Say to those who are of a fearful and hasty heart, Be strong, fear not! Behold, your God will come with vengeance; with the recompense of God He will come and save you.

Matthew 21:22 (Amp)

And whatever you ask for in prayer, having faith and [really] believing, you will receive.

Negative thinking and give up attitudes are examples of the enemy attacking your thoughts; he wants you to have a defeated mentality, which can ultimately destroy you. It is wise to counter attack him by doing our job before the attack even comes.

The next phase for me would be quite challenging. I must tell you, if I did not have a relationship with God, I would not have been alive. Rehab was going well until I had a setback. Something began to go wrong with my left leg. It began to swell uncontrollably and every time I moved, I was in tremendous pain. Papa and my husband came to see me as they did every day; Mama, my paternal grandmother, stayed every night at the hospital and took care of me, even to the point of feeding me. They asked me why I was crying. My husband touched my leg and I screamed! My nurse initially thought I was being dramatic and getting a little lazy because I did not want to work hard but that was not it at all. They ended up stopping my therapy because I was in too much pain.

Later that day, my rehab nurse and the rehab doctor came to inform me that they suspected a blood clot had formed and I needed a deep vein thrombosis ultrasound on my leg. What? A blood clot? No way! Oxygen had been on my legs day and night. I was just taken off it three days ago. I was moving every day during rehab. How could this happen?

Looking in the Face of Death

This dreadfully painful test left me agonizing in pain because the instrument used to detect blood clots had to be pressed deeply along the length and width of my entire leg. After the test, I went back to my room and waited for the results; it was confirmed that blood clots indeed formed so I was put on anticoagulants to stop the clotting. The doctor also put me on total bedrest. Any amount of activity greatly increased the likelihood of the blood clots travelling throughout my body.

While on bedrest, the doctors had the results from the biopsy of the growth that was on my spine. It was September 9, 2003 about 6:00 in the evening when we got a phone call that the neurologist needed to see my immediate family. Here we go again with the "see your family" thing. Apparently, it was very serious. At about 8:15 that evening, the neurologist came in with Dr. Barai, an Oncologist. "Lymphoma Cancer is what you have" was what I heard them say before their words began to fade in my mind. Only God knows where the cancer came from and how I got it. They continued talking, informing me that I would have to receive a series of tests to see if there were any other growths in that area, if the cancer had spread to other areas in my body, if I needed to take chemotherapy and if so, was my heart strong enough to take the chemotherapy.

To say I was devastated was a gross understatement. Stunned, shocked, and speechless was my state of mind as I searched for the words and reasons why I was facing this. Cancer? No, not me. Am I going to die? What stage is it? My babies! My husband! My family! Oh no God! No! I could not even listen to the doctor because the voices inside of me were drowning him out. My husband held my hand and we cried together.

The doctors left to give us some time to process this news. My husband was saying things like "No not you, it should have been me." I said, "Don't say that." Immediately, I heard in my spirit, **"THIS IS NOT UNTIL DEATH!"** Then I remembered something the doctor said, "God is going to use me to kill cancer." Immediately, I wiped my eyes, looked at my husband and said three sentences that were critical in this battle… "I am a fighter. I trust God. I am already healed."

Psalm 118:17 (Amp)

I shall not die but live, and shall declare the works and recount the illustrious acts of the Lord!

Looking in the Face of Death

I was transferred to the oncology ward. When I arrived, my nurse for the evening began to speak nothing but negative words to me. She said things like, "This is horrible; you know you're going to have to take chemotherapy; you will probably lose your hair; you're so young and you can't walk; this is terrible." I could not believe all this was coming out of her mouth. I had just been given a negative report, and then she came to me with a negative response. However, I refused to give in to the venomous words she was speaking. As she left the room to check on other patients, I began to pray with boldness and authority that *no weapon formed against me would prosper* (Isaiah 54:17) and no one was going to steal my confession of faith. I asked God not to allow that nurse in the room ever again. She did not even finish the shift that night and I never saw her again. We have to remember that when we tell God that we are going to believe in Him and not doubt, the enemy will come to challenge our faith with fear.

1 Peter 5:8 (Amp)

Be well balanced, be vigilant and cautious at all times; for that enemy of yours, the devil, roams around like a lion roaring [in fierce hunger], seeking someone to seize upon and devour.

Now I had just confessed the Word, built myself up and here's the enemy trying to get me off track. However, I prayed in faith and decided to withstand the enemy and he fled!

James 4:7 (Amp)

So be subject to God. Resist the devil [stand firm against him], and he will flee from you.

I was very selective about who I allowed around me. I did not need anyone crying and putting me in the grave with their words. When I told my grandmother, Mama Mary Dee, about the diagnosis, it was too much for her to handle so she didn't come around me; her sister was dealing with cancer and it was almost unbearable for her so she couldn't stand to know this was going on with me. I love Mama for that….she did not bring any of the negativity around me.

I went through test after test after test. It was so emotionally draining, but I continued to read my Word to help strengthen me. The doctors reported that there was a nodglin in my chest and three to five percent in the bone marrow. It was Stage 1 Low Grade Non-Hodgkin's Lymphoma. My heart was strong enough to receive chemotherapy and I was told that I would take it for six to eight months. Lord really? Chemotherapy? I had heard so many horror stories about it as well as seen its awful effects. Would I lose so much weight that I would not be recognizable? Oh my God! My hair, it is already really short. How much will I lose? Am I going to be bald? All of these thoughts were racing through my mind.

One of the last tests before treatment was the bone marrow test. They wanted to see how much cancer had gotten to my bones and how invasive it had become (if it was extremely aggressive, I needed to be placed on the bone marrow transplant list). My neighbor in the bed next to me had already warned me that this would be a terribly painful test. The needles were as long as my leg and that they have to go in my hip to do the bone test. Ouch! Dr. Barai told me not to listen to my neighbor. Do not believe what others say.

When I had the test, my husband, the doctor and the nurse were the only ones in the room. He numbed me and started the test; I only felt a little pressure and I thought he was still numbing me because he did not tell me when he started. Once it was over, he began to ask me questions about my favorite movies and just small talk so I'm thinking he was about to start. No! I began to tense up and he said, "I'm done." He purposely did not tell me when he did the procedure. I was not in pain! He said, "I told you don't listen to your neighbor."

The aftermath was the most painful due to soreness. Since I endured that, I believed I could handle chemotherapy. I was told that I would receive a port-a-cathe. This was the device that supplied the chemotherapy; it is placed just below the skin in either the chest or arm and connected to a vein. Dr. Barai stated that chemotherapy would become hard on my veins in my arms, so the port-a-cathe was put on the right side of my chest and it was painful! I had tubes everywhere; because I had blood clots, I was getting my blood drawn every four hours.

Chemotherapy started about two weeks after the diagnosis. I was vomiting, tired, in pain and exhausted with no appetite. I just wanted to sleep to escape the pain and torture. My family was there every step of the way. My husband would leave work and come directly to hospital to be with me. Everyone took turns doing all they could to make sure I was being taken care of while there.

After a few weeks of treatment, Dr. Barai decided it was ok to discharge me from the hospital to go home. He gave Archie and me instructions on how to provide at-home care. Home so soon? I had mixed emotions about his decision. Initially, I thought it was a great idea but then the logistics of being back home concerned me. On one hand, I did like the idea of not being at the hospital and having the opportunity to see my babies and family and friends but on the other hand, I did not think it was safe to be at home without all the essential equipment and staff. Would I heal properly at home? How would I maneuver? I didn't want anything to hinder me getting well because the doctor said if I got any type of minor illness, a cough or slight fever, I had to come back to the hospital; they did not want to risk my progress. I began to have anxiety about going home. I knew I had to attack the spirit of fear so once again, God's Word became my primary and first weapon of choice.

II Timothy 1:7 (Amp)

For God did not give us a spirit of timidity (of cowardice, of craven and cringing and fawning fear), but [He has given us a spirit] of power and of love and of calm and well-balanced mind and discipline and self-control.

I will not fear is what I adamantly told myself through the tears.

My stay at the hospital was eight long weeks, which felt like a lifetime. I was released from the hospital on September 25, 2003, my husband's birthday. When we got outside, everything seemed different. The seasons were different, the air felt different. The outside looked and even smelt different. When I went into the hospital, we were in the summer season. Now, fall was setting in. Nothing seemed familiar anymore. I felt like a foreigner and alien. Life as I had known it was now different. My husband did not understand why I was so distant and not enthusiastic about coming home. It's not that I wasn't happy about coming home. Between all the words of warning from the doctor, me having to relearn how to walk again and the barrage of thoughts of the possibility of having to go back to the hospital, I was fighting fear.

The car ride home was particularly painful, overwhelming, and horrible. It felt like I was on a roller coaster. My husband drove very gently but for me it felt like a roller coaster. With each bump we hit, pain radiated throughout my body.

When we arrived home, the walker and the toilet seat had not yet arrived so that did not make for a pleasant homecoming. "The walker isn't here, so what am I going to do since I can't walk?" is what I began to say to my mother and husband. My mom was at the door; she came to help my husband bring me in the house. Because I could not walk and there was no equipment to assist me, I was literally drug through the door. I screamed the entire distance because the pain was so unbearable. Since I had no muscle mass to support me, I had to use all of my upper body strength to try to support my unmovable legs.

As I got to the top of the stairs, I saw my daughter looking in horror and disbelief. Her tiny face expressed fear and confusion. She looked so helpless but as I saw that beautiful little face at the top of the stairs, I found strength through the pain. God used my daughter to help me make it up the stairs. I finally made it to the room and after that ordeal, I needed to rest. It felt as if I had just finished an intense workout at the gym. As my mom helped me settle in, I began to look around and realized this was the beginning of a new journey.

The next few days were about getting adjusted. I began to focus on moving forward: walking, overcoming this diagnosis of cancer and getting back to the things I loved doing (being a wife and mother, singing, acting, doing hair and makeup). I could not focus on anything or anyone else at that time. That was the problem in the first place… not having balance. I needed to shift my priorities. I had to allow God to be sovereign in my life and allow Him to be first. I had to listen to the Holy Spirit for directions. The old ways of doing and being were no longer an option. My very life was dependent on me making changes, starting now with trusting God and totally relying on Him and His plan. I had to learn how to truly rest in Him more than I have ever done so in my life.

Romans 8:26 (Amp)

So too the [Holy] Spirit comes to our aid and bears us up in our weakness; for we do not know what prayer to offer nor how to offer it worthily as we ought, but the Spirit Himself goes to meet our supplication and pleads in our behalf with unspeakable yearnings and groanings too deep for utterance.

My daughter seemed to be relieved that I was home. Even though I could not fulfill all my duties as a mother, just seeing mommy again seemed to uplift her spirit. She began to look brighter and of course seeing her face was joy and strength for me. My son was about 15 ½ months and just busy. He stayed with my mom and she would bring him to see me daily. My husband and I were living with Papa until our Habitat for Humanity home was completed, and with the 24-hour care that I needed, being there was a tremendous help. My aunt Terri also lived there so between work and helping to take care of me, her life was pretty full. With my husband, my mom, Papa, my aunt and my friends taking turns to care for my needs, everything seemed to work for my family and me.

Looking in the Face of Death

I began chemotherapy again the week after coming home. The office was beautiful. Dr. Barai made sure that every patient was comfortable. The nursing staff treated everyone so warm and gentle; they were extremely patient with us. They made it a little bit easier to come to the office each day to receive these vile treatments. Chemotherapy was four days every other week depending on my blood counts. If my blood counts were up then I had chemotherapy. It my blood counts were down, there was no chemotherapy.

Outside of prayer, nothing can truly prepare anyone for chemotherapy. I felt like I was a zombie every day...no energy, no spunk, unbearable nausea. Lifting a finger felt like I was lifting weights. By the time I felt better, it was time for another round of chemotherapy. The Word kept me going forward when I did not have the energy. I read the Bible on healing every day. I watched Christian television daily to help keep my spirit constantly feasting on the Word of God.

Hebrews 4:12 (Amp)

For the Word that God speaks is alive and full of power [making it active, operative, energizing, and effective]; it is sharper than any two-edged sword, penetrating to the dividing line of the breath of life (soul) and [the immortal] spirit, and of joints and marrow [of the deepest parts of our nature], exposing and sifting and analyzing and judging the very thoughts and purposes of the heart.

The word is alive! It was the power I needed to forge through the most difficult time in my life. Because I was in the fight of my life for my life, I could not afford to have anything negative in my ear gate, eye gate and mouth gate. Every word and every thought was critical so I had to have the Word of God as the only source feeding my spirit. Am I saying do not watch anything else when you are going through? I cannot tell anyone else what to do. I can only tell you what worked for me!

Chapter 5

Turmoil Turned To Triumph

Live to Win

I meditated on His Word nonstop, especially scriptures on healing. You must realize it is a constant battle in the mind; satan was hurling assault after assault against me. The enemy was on one side saying, "ok you're healed, but it's going to come back; you won't see your children grow up, no growing old with your husband. This cancer is going to kill you." Yet I had the Word on the other side and because I fed myself the Word daily, I became strong enough to resist the lies of the devil.

Isaiah 54:17 (Amp)

But no weapon that is formed against you shall prosper, and every tongue that shall rise against you in judgment you shall show to be in the wrong. This [peace, righteousness, security, triumph over opposition] is the heritage of the servants of the Lord [those in whom the ideal Servant of the Lord is reproduced]; this is the righteousness or the vindication which they obtain from Me [this is that which I impart to them as their justification], says the Lord.

Psalm 121 (Amp)

I will lift up my eyes to the hills [around Jerusalem, to sacred Mount Zion and Mount Moriah]—From whence shall my help come? My help comes from the Lord, Who made heaven and earth. He will not allow your foot to slip or to be moved; He Who keeps you will not slumber. Behold, He who keeps Israel will neither slumber nor sleep. The Lord is your keeper; the Lord is your shade on your right hand [the side not carrying a shield].

Turmoil to Triumph

The sun shall not smite you by day, nor the moon by night. The Lord will keep you from all evil; He will keep your life. The Lord will keep your going out and your coming in from this time forth and forevermore.

Psalm 124

If it had not been the Lord Who was on our side—now may Israel say— If it had not been the Lord Who was on our side when men rose up against us, Then they would have quickly swallowed us up alive when their wrath was kindled against us;
Then the waters would have overwhelmed us and swept us away, the torrent would have gone over us; Then the proud waters would have gone over us. Blessed be the Lord, Who has not given us as prey to their teeth! We are like a bird escaped from the snare of the fowlers; the snare is broken, and we have escaped! Our help is in the name of the Lord, Who made heaven and earth.

If I did not build myself up in the Word, I would have allowed the enemy to eventually destroy me with depression. You see, he was trying to attack me about my future…I would not see Amari or Ahmad graduate from high school or see them get married. I would not get back on stage to minister or perform anymore.

Even though I was firm on the fact that I was already healed, I still had anxiety and fear about my future. The enemy saw that is where I struggled so he bombarded my mind with thoughts of not seeing my family and major events in their lives. I found scriptures to counter attack those thoughts.

Psalms 118:6

The Lord is on my side; I will not fear. What can man do to me.

Nahum 1:9

What do ye imagine against the LORD? He will make an utter end: affliction shall not rise up the second time.

These scriptures served as my reminder that cancer could not come back and therefore would not be a factor in my future. This became my confession of faith for my future. I was still taking chemotherapy and not walking yet, so why was I thinking about life years down the road? I knew my healing was already a done deal! I was not wavering because I had already received my healing. My new confession: "It will never come back, my children won't have it, their children won't have it, and their children's children won't have it! This generational curse has been cut off of my bloodline." I had to be strong in my faith so that no matter what it looked like, no matter what the diagnosis sounded like, I believed and stood firm in faith.

Turmoil to Triumph

Hebrews 11:6 (Amp)

But without faith it is impossible to please and be satisfactory to Him. For whoever would come near to God must [necessarily] believe that God exists and that He is the rewarder of those who earnestly and diligently seek Him [out].

Although I endured surgery, rehab and chemotherapy, I had to trust God. The more I read the Word, the more I relied on Him and His faithfulness. As I began to feed my spirt the Word, the stronger my faith became and not only that, I began to have a greater understanding of my authority as His child. I began to say, "No I don't have to accept this sickness. No, I will not die but live and declare His goodness. I will experience life in abundance to the full, until it overflows. I will sing again. I will dance again. This cancer or any other form of cancer will not come back on me." Every day, the Word would rise up in me and caused me to boldly declare my healing.

The enemy was trying to shut me up and keep me from talking and singing because he knows I bring glory and honor to God with my voice. Even while going through all of this, I had found a way to still use my gifts. When I spent those two weeks in rehab, I met many patients. Some had surgery and some were diagnosed with different illnesses. There was one woman in particular who was dealing with MS (Multiple Sclerosis). She was so overwhelmed that she cried almost every day. It was heart wrenching just looking at everyone including myself, and just thinking of how we wanted all of this to be over. We began to do group activities and during two of our sessions, I sang. I had not used my vocal pipes in a little while and I just wanted to uplift everyone, like David did with Saul and the harp. Music can be just as soothing and calming as medicine. As I began to sing, some of the patients began to cry. Many of them began to ask me if I had sang professionally and I began to tell them about me singing in church and the recent musical theatre production.

I felt better that day! I called my mom to bring copies of the music I had recorded a year ago. I gave away three CD's that day. It was then when I undoubtedly realized I was not just a singer doing this for a hobby, but I was born and called to do this. Yes, I had been singing all my life and pursuing things, yes it was a dream of mine, but because I made other choices in my life, I put it on the back burner. Now I realized that God had given me a gift to share and I needed to share it. I felt so fulfilled after that day. Patients were hugging me and we all bonded during that time. It was beautiful.

It was the middle of November and I wanted to go to church. My mom asked me how I felt. I said, "Look, let me get this walker and help me get moving." I believed that through the power of prayer and laying on of hands that I would be made whole again. My mom helped me get dressed and we went to church. As I got closer to church, my expectation increased! I knew once I got around the saints of God, I would feel brand new. I had not been to church since August and I could not wait to get there. As I entered the door, the members began to pour the love of God all over me; they hugged me, encouraged me and were praising God that I was there. I felt His presence and missed being in a corporate anointing like that! As service went on, my pastor at the time, Pastor Shackelford began to ask people to come up for prayer. Since I was not able to stand for a long period of time, my pastor came and asked if he could pray with and for me. I told him about the nodule in the chest and I believed that it was gone and he stood in agreement with me. A week later, Dr. Barai confirmed the tumor was gone! I realized that *God is the same yesterday today and forever* (Hebrews 13:8).

February 2004 had marked six and a half months of chemotherapy treatment. I was so tired of the treatment that I got angry one night, threw that walker, and said this is it! I'm healed and I'm not taking chemotherapy anymore! Now chemotherapy was supposed to last at least 6 to 8 months and if it was not effective, I would be placed on the donor's list for a bone marrow transplant. No, I was not receiving that report. I held fast to the truth of what the Word said…by His stripes, I was healed so my confession was I am healed. The following day I asked Dr. Barai to send me in for an MRI. Well he was already on it. He wanted to send me in for one anyway. After performing tests to see how my body was responding to treatments, the doctors declared that I was cancer free! He only confirmed what I already knew and being as though it was already declared by God that I was healed, it was merely a matter of time that my healing manifested! Dr. Barai said my spirit made me whole and that my cheerful attitude carried me through this painful process.

Proverbs 17:22 (Amp)

A happy heart is good medicine and a cheerful mind works healing, but a broken spirit dries up the bones.

Turmoil to Triumph

Although I no longer had to take chemotherapy, I was to still see him once a month to do bloodwork and continue with physical therapy. My thought was if God removed the cancer, He would heal my legs so that I can walk without the aid of anything. My legs and feet still felt heavy. I continued to do physical therapy at home three times a week. It was tough because I was using muscles that had not been used in a few months. Nevertheless, I persevered through it all because I knew I was getting better each time I endured the difficulties.

One morning while watching Christian television, a popular healing televangelist was praying and said that a woman on a cane had just been healed. My mom was sitting there and when she heard it, she jumped up and said that is you baby. I believed God that it was I and did not dwell on it anymore.

I went to the bathroom and when I came out my mom said my husband was waiting to take me to the doctor. I was so focused on getting downstairs so Archie would not fuss at me about being late that I forgot the cane! My husband asked me where the cane was, and at that point, I realized that God answered my prayer. I laughed and just marveled at the awesomeness of God! There was no feeling that a miracle happened, no sensation, no outward indicator that we are so conditioned to get. You know how you church folks are…. Oh, I felt that. I got chills. I felt the anointing. I saw five birds form a cross in the sky; that is my confirmation! The man of God spoke the word, I believed it and God did the rest. From that day forward, I never used a cane or walker again!

My steps were not completely smooth and fluid as they used to be but I was able to walk without any assistance. This was a miracle in and of itself! I continued therapy; I was determined to have that stride again! I will have my model gait again! DON'T JUDGE ME! That was my confession and my faith. ☺

I was told that the numbness and tingling in my legs and feet would remain for a while; I would just have to deal with it. Now you know that did not sit well with me. I was not receiving that report. I decided to go on a 30-day plant based fast at the recommendation of a family member who was a holistic doctor. I figured that if he could look that good and be in such great shape at the age of 80, I should listen to what he had to say. He instructed me to only consume raw organic fruits and vegetables. Juices and smoothies were the only things I drank and ate for that time. Initially, I was a bit tired and irritable because I was not eating what I wanted but I soon got over that because this life-giving food was helping me. After 30 days, there were dramatic changes in me. I was able to come off all my medications, my walking became normal, all the numbness and tingling was gone and I lost 30 pounds! God is awesome! A month later, I was wearing high heels! My healing had progressed so well that in November 2004, I started a dance school at my church teaching ballet, tap, and modern dance. To God be the glory!

God not only restored my health, but every other part of my life was healed and restored. God worked a miracle in my heart and healed the emotional hurts; I completely released every worry, care and concern to Him. I no longer held onto the hurt. This brought healing and restoration to my marriage. Even when we got hit with another devastating blow when our Habitat for Humanity home was burnt down, Archie and I stood in faith together and believed God to get us through that ordeal. My clientele was restored. God opened up many doors in ministry as well as in arts and entertainment to share His love. To God be ALL the glory!

Just as I chose to live, so too do I pray that you make that same decision to live! John 10:10 (Amp) says *the thief comes only in order to steal and kill and destroy. I came that they may have and enjoy life, and have it in abundance (to the full, till it overflows).*

Endnotes

1. http://www.biblica.com/en-us/bible/online-bible/msg/hebrews/12/msg/

CONFESSION

Father, I give You all the praise, the glory and the honor. You are a mighty and powerful God. I thank You for total restoration over my body. Sickness and disease has no power over me. I decree and declare that I am healed by Your stripes and I walk in total victory. The voice of the enemy is silenced and I believe the Word of God. I shall live and not die. No matter what it feels like, I will stand on the Word of God. Healing belongs to me in Jesus' name, Amen!

DAILY AFFIRMATIONS

I forgive and let go.

I have a clean heart and a renewed spirit.

I walk and live by faith.

I speak life and not death.

I cast down all fear and doubt.

Affliction will not rise against me again.

The enemy has no authority over my life.

I feed my spirit the Word of God daily.

I believe and receive the Word of God

I AM HEALED AND THAT IS THE FINAL ANSWER.

PRAYER OF SALVATION

You too can experience the healing and restoration from God. Through salvation, God provides not only the escape from hell but also redemption from sin and deliverance from destitution.

The Bible says "God so loved the world that He gave His only Son, that whoever believes in Him shall not perish but have eternal life (John 3:16). This is a free gift that can never be earned. Your only job is to confess, believe and receive for those who call on the name of the Lord shall be saved (Romans 10:13).

If you are ready to receive salvation, allow me the pleasure to lead you through the prayer of salvation. Say this prayer:

Lord Jesus,

I believe you are the Son of God. I believe You died on the cross for my sins and was raised from the dead. I know I am a sinner and I ask for Your forgiveness. I ask you to be my Lord and Savior. Thank you for giving me a new life! Amen.

Biography

Altovise Ferguson is a native of Gary, Indiana. She began her career as a dancer, under the instruction of the late Corine Morse Williams. It was Ms. Corine that realized Altovise possessed the gift of singing. Soon she discovered the world of modeling at John Robert Powers. After graduating from Emerson Visual & Performing Arts High School in 1994, she went on to pursue a career in cosmetology.

Altovise became an actress with the West Side Theatre Guild. She starred in the stage plays Joseph & The Amazing Technicolor Dreamcoat and Guys & Dolls. She also starred in a series of the Lyrics stage plays as well as the films Guilded Six Bits and The Ballad of Sadie Hawkins.

She has ministered on Word Network and Trinity Broadcasting Network. Altovise was the opening act for the 2009, 2013 and 2015 Epitome Awards in Dallas, TX. She also sang during the 2012 inauguration of Gary, Indiana's mayor, the honorable Karen Freeman-Wilson. In 2012, Altovise was a Top 20 finalist during the Shine FM Radio Station singing contest and awarded the Gary, Indiana Stellar Award for Female Vocalist of the Year.

Her community outreach includes being a guest presenter for youth empowerment workshops and for various parent advocacy issues.

Altovise is married to Archie L. Ferguson Jr. and she is the mother to three children.

Follow Altovise to stay updated with her latest ministry events, concerts, tour dates and much more:

    Website: www.altoviseferguson.com

    Facebook: AltoviseFerguson1

    Twitter: @AltoviseF

    Instagram: @AltoviseF

    Periscope: @AltoviseF

You can find her latest single, "Something Out of Nothing" at all major online music outlets.

For book signing events and/or speaking engagements e-mail: publishinglife@yahoo.com or call 219-730-7621.

www.ingramcontent.com/pod-product-compliance
Lightning Source LLC
Chambersburg PA
CBHW070550300426
44113CB00011B/1854